BRINGING UP YOUR TEENAGE DAUGHTER

In the WhatsApp Age

Rupa Chatterjee

V&S PUBLISHERS

Published by:

V&S PUBLISHERS

F-2/16, Ansari road, Daryaganj, New Delhi-110002
☎ 23240026, 23240027 • *Fax:* 011-23240028
Email: info@vspublishers.com • *Website:* www.vspublishers.com

Regional Office : Hyderabad
5-1-707/1, Brij Bhawan (Beside Central Bank of India Lane)
Bank Street, Koti, Hyderabad - 500 095
☎ 040-24737290
E-mail: vspublishershyd@gmail.com

Branch Office : Mumbai
Jaywant Industrial Estate, 1st Floor–108, Tardeo Road
Opposite Sobo Central Mall, Mumbai – 400 034
☎ 022-23510736
E-mail: vspublishersmum@gmail.com

Follow us on:

© **Copyright:** V&S PUBLISHERS
Edition 2018

Printed at Repro Knowledgecast Limited, Thane

❧ ✳ ✳ ❧

Dedicated to

"My Mother, Gauri Banerji
My Daughters, Romira & Ronita
And
Grand daughter, Riya"

❧ ✳ ✳ ❧

Preface

$\mathscr{T}$he winds of change sweeping into our society have brought many new avenues and opportunities are opening up to our daughters, which were not there even a decade back. Along with economic liberalization, the spread of education and the growth of television, new doors of opportunity are available to our daughters. From one Kiran Bedi there are now hundreds of them in the police forces, army, navy and air force. A girl of Indian origin in the United States, Kalpana Chawla, was part of the space programme. Reality TV has crept into our drawing rooms and parents from small towns of India are allowing their young daughters to participate in song and dance competitions or beauty pageants, which would not have happened even five years ago. For many mothers, not only is the *ghoongat* out, but even they are getting into jeans and skirts and thumbing their nose at convention. The divorce rate is up, careers are paramount and motherhood is taking a back seat in the present scheme of things. Changes are taking place very swiftly, but it is necessary to step back and take a look at what we are doing and what awaits us in the future. While society is changing, human nature and biology remains, constant. The instinct to find a partner and nurture comes up as nature designed it to do.

Thus, the question arises is how much should we change as parents and as daughters to survive in the present scenario? If life is all about balance and juggling multiple roles and responsibilities, then my revised edition will try to update the reader on the new situations arising out of our changing society and how we can raise and help our daughters in the present day.

Rupa Chatterjee

Contents

Introduction

$\mathcal{U}$ntil the last three decades women throughout the world were placed in a special category – to be protected, cosseted, respected, revered, or discriminated against and exploited, as the situation warranted.

Till the mid-1960s, women all over the world were expected to fulfil their designated traditional roles in society which encompassed, as the Germans put it, "children, the kitchen and the church". Although history is full of instances of learned women and powerful queens from Vedic India to Victorian England, women by and large played a secondary role in society. A woman's ultimate aim was to have a 'good' marriage, as wealth, power and social prestige all emanated from the man and his status in society. The concept of a woman having her own identity and independent status simply did not exist.

After the First World War, when women were forced to help in the war effort and even take up jobs in factories, the Women's Suffragette Movement in the United States and England sought to obtain the right to vote. Despite their image of being 'advanced' and 'modern', women in Western societies were as dominated upon as their sisters elsewhere. During the Middle Ages, though chivalry was the order of the day, knights going on Crusades bound their wives with a chastity belt. Even as men fought duels to maintain the honour of their ladies, clerics asked, "Do women have souls?"

Even today, in many so-called modern and civilised cultures there are separate norms for men and women. For example, even in 21st century Japan, a girl cannot ascend the throne. The

7

Japanese ruler, believed to be a direct descendant of the Sun God, can only be male. In many Western countries, men and women do not receive equal pay for equal work and in Switzerland, women had not received the right to vote until the early 1990s.

For many centuries, the pattern of women's lives remained the same. Education for them was not considered important. Beauty, docility, domestic skills, obedience and patience were necessary virtues that had to be cultivated. Divorce was virtually unheard of and strong social strictures ensured that marriage was a permanent bond.

Although the Women's Liberation Movement of the 1960s, along with the emancipating effect of the birth control pill, forced a radical change in Western societies, in other parts of the world the effect has not been so dramatic. Yes, women are more educated and seek to utilise their education to become professionals and financially independent, but the home and family are still given importance, particularly in Indian society. Since India moves in several centuries at the same time, there are still many in the remote areas who bring up the girl-child as had been done over the millennium, with few concessions to modernity.

But in general, as the Taliban experience in Afghanistan has proved, the clock cannot be turned back to the medieval ages – some concessions have to be made to modernity and the winds of change are seeping in, no matter how slowly.

In order to bring up one's daughter in 21st century India, it is necessary to do what Indian society is known for, which is to achieve a fusion between the best of tradition and modernity, so that our daughters can achieve a pivotal role in the future of both the country and our family system. Individuals cannot function in a vacuum, so it is essential that the girl-child be brought up in a way that combines the best from the past in order to fulfill the challenges of the unknown future, without compromising on one's values and traditions.

This book seeks to offer balanced guidelines on the best ways of bringing up a daughter in present-day India. Thus, a broad gamut of topics have been touched upon. Sometimes the reader may find that the author is judgmental, at other times, liberal. This is because in today's fast-changing environment a rigid stance may be counterproductive, since girls are now being subjected to many influences that were not prevalent in an earlier era, such as excessive peer pressure, exposure to the media and the influence of the fashion industry.

Thus, it requires a great deal of maturity and tactful handling to exercise some influence over our children and to guide them in successfully tackling the multifarious roles that they face in the present world – as daughters, students, career women, wives, mothers and mothers-in-law. I do hope this book achieves that objective in some small measure.

Rupa Chatterjee

Handling
Teenagers

Adolescence marks a period of rapid and profound change in both the body and mind. Coping with adolescence and its attendant physical and psychological changes makes the teenage years a trying time for both parents and children. Children become more vocal about their opinions, their expectations and their desire for freedom. Often they adopt a collision path with elders, arguing and questioning until parents lose patience. I remember that one year our American fiend walked in and after some time said, "I have two teenagers in the house!," as though it were some calamity.

In fact, teenagers have an in-built desire to rebel and rail against any authoritarian stance adopted by parents. Being older in age and hopefully wiser – having passed through a similar stage themselves – parents should not only "play it cool", but also avoid reading out the riot act at every juncture. Avoid making too many rules and regulations. Above all, try to avoid rigid, unbending stances; these only foster rebellion.

This does not mean that parents should not exercise their judgement or lay down certain broad parameters of behaviour. In fact, teenagers expect that certain norms and standards be adhered to. Parents should adopt a pleasant and consensual approach to all matters

11

rather than one of confrontation and expect blind obedience from their children. Times have changed and unquestioning obedience is something that vanished with the 19th century. Parents should lay down a few basic guidelines and ensure that these are adhered to, rather than make too many irritating regulations.

Teenagers require support, love and guidance from their parents but not constant policing. In fact, preparing your child to fly is part of the parenting cycle and this can be seen in the bird family and among four legged animals too. Therefore, by letting go gradually one would get a far better response if one dealt with teenagers like responsible adults, rather than irresponsible, unreliable juveniles. If one has built up a good rapport during the childhood years, the teenage years will certainly pass off more smoothly.

Traditional psychologists of the 19th century made out that the period of adolescence was marked by a period of dark, angry turmoil into adulthood. However, Dr Daniel Offer, an American psychiatrist, re-examined this concept of the teenage years during the 1960s and asserted that the idea that the teen years are necessarily a period of rebellion and madness has misled many.

During teenage years, family bickering increases due to issues like schoolwork, dress, friends, outings and household chores. A cogent explanation comes from the work of the Swiss psychologist Jean Piaget, who proved that children did not have the capacity for abstract and analytical thinking until the teenage years. It is the arrival of this capacity that enables them to question their parents' thinking.

An associate professor of education, psychology and pediatrics', Judith Smetana, contends that concentrating on the development of a child's ability to think logically is not useful in elucidating family relationships. According to her research, there are two fundamentally different worldviews at the core of family conflict. While adolescents tend to see much of their behaviour as a "personal" matter, affecting no one but themselves and therefore up to them entirely, their parents tend to stand for "conventional thinking", which sees society's rules and expectations as primary.

This dichotomy leads to commonplace clashes regarding dress, studies, cleanliness of the teenager's rooms and so on.

Smetana charts the thinking pattern of a teenager in the following manner. A child of 12 or 13 generally has little time for conventions when it comes to family issues. Between 14 and 16 years, the teenager realises that conventions are ways in which society regulates itself. Between 16 and 18 years there is again a period of rejecting conventions, but more thoughtfully. Between 18 and 25 years, conventions are once again seen as playing an admirable role in facilitating the business of society. This is why, usually, by the age of 15 or 16 years quarrelling subsides and is replaced by a period in which the family "negotiates" issues such as staying out late, going out with the opposite sex and so on.

Parents who try to exert too much control find it impossible to yield in a conflict where their teenaged children are trying to establish their own identities. In this trying period where teenagers try to express their individuality, even as they want to maintain a close and caring relationship with the parents, the parents have to be positive and caring in order to tide over this difficult period.

In cases where parents adopt the stance of being the last bastions of conservatism, or where they are harsh and judgmental, there is a great danger of alienation. When faced with a consistently negative and hostile environment at home, children will be driven towards their peer group. Peer pressure and camaraderie often lead towards anti-social behaviour, drug addiction, smoking, alcohol and sex. It is only through compassion, love, understanding and constant communication that parents can exert influence during this trying time of physical and psychological changes in young adults.

By giving the teenager some measure of freedom, privacy and respect as a young adult, parents may be in a better position to avoid teenage rebellion.

Some Handy Tips

1. Early bonding – the closer the relationship in the pre-teen years, the easier it is during the teenage years. Confidence and self-esteem should be built up by listening to them, so that they do not have to do outlandish things to gain your attention.

2. Share decision-making, as parenting does not mean being a dictator. By offering your child choices and including them in decisions, such as the decoration and cleanliness of their room and the like, it enables them to get a feeling of participation in the household.

3. Understand growing pains – don't exert your will over them for every trivial issue but keep a grip on the main ones. Do not peer over their shoulder at every stage but give them space and privacy.

4. Keep the lines of communication open on all topics, including sex, at all times. Make them a part of your lives by seeking their opinion regarding your clothes, make-up etc, so that they feel valued.

5. Make mealtimes a happy hour for family bonding and light conversation. Do not chastise them or broach unpleasant topics while eating.

6. Know your children's friends and encourage them to come over for meals occasionally or simply to drop in. Avoid harsh criticism of their friends. Peer pressure is a reality at this stage, as children around the age of 15 like what their friends are doing. The group that moves together does almost everything together, such as going out for movies or parties and liking the same music and film stars.

7. Set reasonable limits for going out, returning home after a party, going out for movies and studying. Adopt a balance between unrestrained behaviour and a jail warden's mindset. Share your worries with your teenaged children and convince them that your concern for them arises from love, not distrust. In this regard, the cellphone has become

an essential part of life. Avoid disturbing your children when they are out with their friends, but keep in touch through messages for convenience and their safety.

8. Remember your own teenaged years and understand that your child may take a bite of the forbidden fruit! See that accurate information about alcohol, drugs, sex and AIDS is given well in advance, through appropriate reading material and frank discussions.

9. Patience, understanding, love and compassion go a long way towards harmonious family relationships. Rocked by internal changes, your teenaged child needs this the most at the appropriate time. Remember this is a transitional phase and it won't last forever; so keep your cool.

Mistakes to Avoid

1. Do not be a control freak and monitor every minute of the child's day. I was recently shocked when a mother, who happens to be a teacher in a top Delhi school, told me that she had come to my house for lunch after locking her teenaged daughter in the house! She had also taken the precaution of locking the room where the TV and the computer/Internet connection was! As it is, teenagers crave for freedom. If they feel that their parents are like jail wardens they will be driven to escape this claustrophobic atmosphere. Children on whom unreasonable curbs are imposed thrive in rebelling against authority.

2. Avoid harsh criticism and a judgmental attitude. Teenagers are just learning how to cope with life – assist them, rather than damage their self-confidence with a carping, critical attitude.

3. Do not try to compete with them. The fact that there is a teenage child indicates you have grown older. Don't try to fight the years by dressing in tank tops and having a perm so that people ask, "Which college do you study in?" While today's society demands that everyone should look young and

fit, don't try to look and behave like a teenager and come into conflict with your teenage children who see a father or mother's attempt to dress and behave like them as a matter of embarrassment.There are other parents who are enrolling in social networking sites such as "Facebook" in order to keep an eye on their children, much to their chagrin.

Clinical psychologist Dr Ashima Puri asserts: "Sharing and caring with authority is what the child's usual expectation from a parent-child relationship is. Even though parents would like to act young, some discrimination should be exercised. They should realise that their role involves a lot of maturity and understanding. They are seen as 'guides' and not as 'peers'. Also, there is the danger of an unconscious, underlying competition developing between parent and child."

This is especially true when a mother is slim, good looking and sophisticated and her daughter is a plump, gauche and acne-faced 14-year-old. Adolescence is the time when children require the maximum guidance, but in a subtle manner. A boy would hate to be hugged in front of his friends for fear of being labelled 'Mama's boy'. At this time adults must behave like adults so that they can guide their teenaged children into adulthood. Most teenagers disapprove and are embarrassed by pony-tailed dads and mini-skirted moms who shriek, giggle and act like teeny-boppers!

In conclusion, given below are some points made by young adolescents of South Asia, who held a conference in 1998, during which they took out a document that recorded their opinions and feelings about the world around them.

Voices of the Adolescents of South Asia

Preamble

We adolescents are not only conscious of our rights but we also feel responsible for moving away from the "me" decade in which we are living, to a decade when adolescents will prove to be an important human resource for the betterment of the region. We pledge to make this a reality.

Our Perspectives

- We feel neglected, and so we need more attention, care and support from all.

- We feel we do not have the right to make our own choices, after knowing all the alternatives – choices relating to our careers, our friends, movements and life partners.

- We greatly lack proper and correct information and guidance, especially relating to our physiological and psychological changes.

- We are not allowed to express our emotions and ourselves.

- We are treated as immature persons. We desire to share responsibilities and prove ourselves.

- We are not given ample opportunities to ascertain our individuality.

- We feel that the dreams and aspirations of our parents should not be imposed on us.

Parents Can You Hear Us?

- We need you to listen to us – to our dreams, our experiences, our explanations, our insecurities and our achievements.

- Give us your time – you gave us life, now we want your time.

- Be our friends.

- Understand us.

- Don't hide things from us, especially when they are related to us.

- Give us the privacy and the space to grow.

- We prefer openness and encouragement to pressures and threats.

17

These were the emotions expressed by young people, not only from India, but also from neighbouring countries such as Nepal and Bangladesh, all of whom were from different socio-economic backgrounds. Parents would do well to keep these points in mind when dealing with their teenage daughters/sons.

Michael Jackson's song "They Don't Really Care About Us" is a virtual anthem for teenagers, most of whom, at some point or another feel alienated from their parents. Therefore give your teenager, who is a bundle of confusion, disturbed emotions and insecurity lots of love, time and understanding and harmony at home will be easy to maintain.

❈ ❈ ❈

Educating
Your Daughter

$\mathcal{I}$n the past, women's education became a casualty to social constraints. The situation is gradually changing. The female literacy rate that was 7.93% in 1951 has risen to 54.16% in the 2001 Census. This is indeed gratifying.

In educating a girl, one is improving the lot of the family, for the girl will be able to provide better health, hygiene and nutrition to the family. Her education can invigorate adult education in a joint family, bring down the rate of illiteracy, thereby stimulating educational consciousness and civic sense among family members. At the macro level, educating a girl leads to socio-economic development of the nation.

In ancient India education of girls had a significant place in society, but with the passage of time and changing circumstances, social evils such as *purdah* and the dowry system came in. When social reformers of the 19th century sought to revitalise Indian society and rescue it from the morass into which it had sunk, they all advocated women's education – right from Raja Ram Mohan Roy and Dayanand Saraswati to Sister Nivedita.

There are two aspects when one talks of education. The first pertains to academics and the basic skill of reading, writing and arithmetic. With the passage of a Bill that declares Education as a Fundamental Right, even the poorest of the poor girl-child in a remote village of this vast country will hopefully have access to some kind of education. Many state governments have special educational plans and programmes for the girl child in which

19

school fees are waived and books and uniforms are provided in order to retain them in school. The *"Ladli"* scheme developed by the Delhi government is one such programme, as the girl child often has to opt out of going to school due to domestic work or lack of finance.

In elite sections of society, the education of a girl is being given equal importance and with the facilitation of student loans, even those not so well off can access higher education, including Medicine, Engineering and Management.

The other component of educating a daughter pertains to certain qualities that are valued in our culture, certain social etiquettes that she must be taught and her role as a transmitter of culture and tradition. Part of the education of a daughter also relates to her ability to dress appropriately, depending on the situation.

Early School Days

A girl-child is a big responsibility, as her safety is always a prime concern for parents. With a floating population of migrant workers, drug addicts, alcoholics, perverts and eve-teasers on the roads, instances of child abuse have been steadily on the rise. Thus all measures must be taken to safeguard your daughter. Unfortunately, she has to be protected even from relations and neighbours, who have been often guilty of child abuse.

● Be very careful about how your child goes to school, who picks her up and who drops her.

● If you pick her up and drop her yourself, it is fine. However, if someone else is entrusted with the job, s/he should be very reliable.

● If the child goes by school bus, she should be picked up promptly from the bus stand.

20

- Instruct the child never to go home with an unknown person, even if the person says that he has been sent by 'Mummy' or 'Daddy'.

- Teach your child never to accept any food and drink, including sweets, toffees or chocolates, from strangers.

The Middle Years (Between 10 and 17)

When your daughter is older, she is still innocent, but it is easier to explain things to her. She should be alerted to the fact that no one should be allowed to touch her body and that she should not remain alone with any male within the school premises. She should also be cautioned against eating from any particular vendor hawking outside the school premises everyday. It has been found that unscrupulous vendors sometimes lace their products with small amounts of drugs, which results in children unwittingly getting addicted to this.

It is only through loving bonds built up in early childhood that one can exert some influence over the child to counter peer pressure and other factors that assume importance during the growing years. A child should genuinely feel that her mother is her well-wisher and that she will receive understanding and sympathy, rather than admonition and disapproval, when she makes a mistake. One should remember one's own childhood and all the mischief one once indulged in! Moreover, every generation received disapproval from their elders for their ways and this trend will continue as long as humans exist.

Mothers should make it a point to be aware of their daughter's close friends, as they exert great influence at this stage. Encourage your daughter to bring her friends over from time to time so that you also get to know her group.

Children in middle and high school often want to bunk school and go out together for movies or an outing. Play along with this desire for some time and ensure that you know where they are going. If you can, give your daughter a cell phone for the duration of the outing so that you are in touch. Many children board the school bus, but go off with their friends, often from the opposite sex, before they reach school and parents are none the wiser. There is no foolproof method of monitoring one's children; hence the only way is to build up a reservoir of trust and common sense which would see them through the unstable years.

The College Days

If the school years were difficult, then the college years could be nightmarish for those parents who are unable to accept that their daughters are growing and have to be given some independence. This is particularly difficult for conservative fathers, who want to exercise absolute control.

One mother, sent away her only daughter to study outside their hometown as she knew that there would be unpleasant fireworks between her rebellious daughter and her conservative father on a daily basis – over her dress, friends, studies, partying and going out. She made this sacrifice at considerable cost to herself, but she rationalised that it would be better than having an unpleasant and violent scene on her hand everyday.

In fact, in India education is not the great leveller that it is expected to be. A man may be highly educated, but he carries with him his childhood values, standards and baggage. With economic advancement, one puts one's children in elite schools where they adopt new norms, but the father is unable to outgrow his childhood constraints. When he tries to impose these on his children, his attempts are met with resentment by the children who find him conservative and anachronistic.

Another pitfall of parenting in India, apart from overbearing supervision, is the tendency to lecture the young. In order to make up for long absences, parents – fathers in particular – feel that they are failing in their duty unless they harangue their children with advice whenever they meet. Children resent this and are non-receptive, so the entire purpose is lost.

While we do not want our children to be rudderless and excessively independent like in the West, where they may move out of the parental home at 16, there is no need to ram unnecessary advice down our children's throats, at a stage when they are trying to work out things for themselves and are particularly unreceptive.

The Hostel Years

Very often parents have no option but to send their children to other cities for higher studies. Some children go off at the school level itself, though this is not so common, as boarding schools have now become very expensive. At the school level, there is ample supervision, but the child does suffer from pangs of homesickness, craving for home food and the company of family members.

At the college or post-graduate level, institutional supervision is limited. Not all students get a seat in the hostel, so two or three friends may get together and rent a room, sharing the work and the expenses. Parents may help the child settle down initially, but ultimately there is no option but to leave the child on her own. One can only hope and pray that all the childhood bonding and indoctrination may now help theri daughter steer clear of drugs, smoking, drinking and promiscuous behaviour. Many children indulge in these activities purely to shock or to draw attention. A well-balanced child who was the recipient of a great deal of affection and attention will be less prone to indulge in these activities. At the same time, one has to be vigilant that the peer group does not lace some food or drink with drugs or alcohol in order to engineer a fall from grace.

As for indulging in promiscuous behaviour with the opposite sex, apart from the danger of disease, including AIDS, one should emphasise that the transience of superficial liaisons will only leave one with feelings of guilt, rejection and low self-esteem. One's body and mind cannot remain untouched by a casual sexual encounter or .relationship, hence one should be very judicious and mindful before indulging in physical relationships.

23

While on the subject of premarital sex, a recent survey revealed that the average age for losing one's virginity in India is around 23 years. This is heartening, as in Western countries, especially North America, those who do not shed their virginity by the mid-teens are panic-stricken! Yet in those countries there is a virgin movement which is growing, after having experimented with casual sex for many decades.

❀ ❀ ❀

A Daughter's Socio-cultural and Sartorial Education

At one time, in most societies, including India, the primary concern with one's daughter was her marriage. Saving for her dowry, bringing her up correctly for the 'real' life at her *sasural* and ensuring that she looked beautiful were virtually an obsession with parents. Times have changed. Today, education is also given importance, but marriage nevertheless retains a predominant place in her upbringing.

In some families influenced by liberal Western thinking, there are efforts to bring up a daughter exactly as one would a son. This is particularly true of those families where there are no sons and the parents turn their daughters into substitute sons. Thus, you have daughters becoming engineers, police officers, pilots and so on. Today from spaceships to submarines and laboratories to stock-broking, the sky is literally no longer the limit for a woman in the professional world.

Despite her presence in the work sphere, the Indian woman has not lost her innate grace and become a hybrid species like her Western counterpart. An Indian girl still tries to combine her professional and domestic life in such a way that neither suffers. Many are staying home to nurture small children, then rejoining the workforce after the age of 40. Others are adjusting by starting lucrative ventures from home such as freelance writing, editing, home catering, chocolate making, running beauty parlours, crèches and so on.

However, problems may now be around the corner as globalisation brings in a new and compulsive work culture and obsessive consumerism, where status, pay packets and material possessions replace human values. Some couples are compromising by becoming DINKs – Double Income No Kids. Such couples are so absorbed in their profession and each other that they have no place for kids and a family in their lives.

Thanks to many such influences, there is a steady rise in divorce rates as women are no longer financially dependent on men and do not wish to languish in dead-end relationships. Tolerance, compromise and patience are at a low ebb. In particular, tolerance for the endless carping criticism of in-laws is at a very low ebb, with many marriages failing on account of interference from in-laws.

One can only hope that the next generation of 21st century daughters will not be dazzled by career options and including everything else. For those who miss out on the benefits of family life, there is a price to pay. Scientific findings confirm that if a woman does not fulfill her biological function of motherhood in time, she could be beset with all kinds of physical problems, including cancer.

Your Daughter at Home

Apart from school education, a mother has to involve her daughter in some other home activities. For example, during festivals you should instruct your daughter about religious and festive rituals, why they are performed and why she needs to participate.

You should teach your daughter the norms of Indian hospitality, which include making adequate food when guests are invited, ensuring that everyone has begun eating or has already eaten before the hostess commences and that all guests are made to feel welcome and comfortable. Besides, she should also know how to greet elders respectfully and make them feel at home when they come over.

Also, encourage your daughter to practice self-control in all matters – eating, shopping and acquiring.

For daughters who have studied and lived abroad, it is imperative to teach them Indian ground rules of entertaining friends and peers. For instance, if an American, European or Australian friend says, "Let's go out for lunch", it means that both will pay for their own meals. In India, however, the person who extends the invitation makes the payment.

If food is sent from someone else's house, the container is not returned empty but filled with some food item as well. If nothing is available at short notice, a bowl of sugar could be given in lieu.

As regards clothes, traditional dresses have been making way for bare-all, figure-hugging Western clothes. These dresses may be suitable for the disco or teenage parties, but are inappropriate at temples, *puja pandals* and even weddings – a fact parents should put across to their children. However, parents are sometimes so dazzled by the modernity of their offspring that they do not exercise their better judgement. But rather than having to impose a dress code for selected functions and festivals, it is preferable if the children are made to understand the importance of wearing or not wearing certain outfits.

A friend's daughter who is extremely fair chose to wear shorts on a visit to South India. Rural India is still highly conservative and people stared open-mouthed, wondering whether some film star or model had come on a visit. Such exposure in a rural environment is positively unsafe and inadvisable, particularly when visiting temples. One needs to dress appropriately, especially at places of worship.

In bringing up one's daughter, therefore, it is not enough to concentrate only on her academic qualifications. There is also the need to sensitize her to norms and traditions of acceptable social behaviour. While going to a disco demands a different dress code, so too one must dress according to the environment and occasion as a lot is determined by what one wears.

❋ ❋ ❋

Some New Hazards of
Bringing Up a Daughter

$\mathcal{G}$oing back in time, it would be evident that families always regarded the upbringing and protection of a daughter as a problem. At one stage, a daughter was linked to family 'honour' in the West and *izzat* in the East, so she had no option but to tread the straight and narrow path to maintain the family name.

Today, rigid social divisions have crumbled across the world and individuals have greater freedom to pursue their own interests, desires and choices rather than merely fulfill family expectations. Urban living has given the individual a great degree of anonymity and privacy compared to rural living, where everyone knows everyone in the community and individuals are still expected to conform to set norms.

Despite the relative anonymity of urban living, people nevertheless build up their own relationships in which they and their children as well as their activities are known to others. As times change, however, so do the problems faced by people. Likewise, parents have to tackle a new set of problems while bringing up their daughters.

Case Study

It is really not advisable to do what my friend Usha, a teacher in a public school, does to her daughter, particularly when Usha goes out. Usha is determined that her daughter should excel in studies so that she can go abroad. Hence, when she has to go out, Usha ensures that rooms that have the phone, television, music system and the computer/ Internet are all locked! I was scandalised when I first heard this instance of utter lack of parental trust – that too by a teacher!

I was therefore curious to see the results of such strictness and was not surprised to find that Usha's daughter had a sour disposition and cribbing nature.

Today, as never before, the information explosion and the mass media have entered our lives in a way that simply cannot be wished away. Nor is it possible to isolate one's children from such influences. For example, the Internet can be accessed through a friend's computer or from cyber cafes. These new threats and external influences must be faced squarely and tackled, rather than being swept under the carpet by not having cable TV, a computer or Internet access. Children should be kept occupied with other activities rather than becoming couch potatoes.

However, children should be allowed some access to computers and the television, as all aspects of these modern amenities are not bad, particularly in terms of information dissemination and education. There are channels such as National Geographic, Animal Planet and Discovery that are very informative for children. Monitor what they see casually, not like some authoritarian dictator.

Boyfriends and the Opposite Sex

India has always been a conservative country and free mixing between the sexes has been restricted to certain echelons of society.

Girls' schools and colleges are located in every town in the country so that parents could enroll their daughters for education in a suitable environment, where she would be taught only by women and not have to intermingle with members of the opposite sex. As a girl's reputation precedes her to the in-laws' home, parents were reluctant to expose their daughter to the company of other young men, lest emotional and other complications spoil her reputation. Therefore, segregation in schools, colleges, hospitals, trains and buses has existed and still continues to exist in India.

Thus the concept of one's daughter having boyfriends, studying in a co-educational school or college and going on dates is still anathema to a majority of Indian parents. This is particularly true for school-going children. Part of the reservation stems from the fact that adults realise that during the vulnerable period of adolescence, children's emotions are raw and rarely balanced enough to deal with the ups and downs of a relationship, let alone with the opposite sex. It is the zeal to protect one's child from pain and suffering that leads parents to impose restrictions on mixing with the opposite sex. Considering the rising numbers seeking psychiatric help to tackle depression, low self-esteem, eating disorders and suicidal tendencies, one can appreciate and understand their position.

In the West, free mixing between the sexes commences quite early, even at nine or ten. Children often stay on their own once they are 16. Alone and insecure, half child and half adult, they are too proud to ask for help from their parents and thus look to relationships with the opposite sex as a source of affection and help. Earlier, Western parents too were strict and conservative and monitored adolescent relationships. However, changes in the social fabric and societal rules regarding romance, marriage, children and divorce have undergone a transformation so that adolescents no longer get that kind of protection abroad.

An Indian girl, on the other hand, is overprotected and cosseted. The extended family environment ensures there is no dearth of affection. Of late, however, experts have been shocked to find that

Indian children too are getting into relationships with the opposite sex as early as Class VIII. This means some begin experimenting around the age of 13 or 14, when they themselves are unsure where the relationship will lead.

Added to all this is the rosy image of love in the media, books, films, advertisements, and a narcissistic explosion of being obsessed with one's looks and figure, all of which leads to early sexual activity, abortions, emotional upheavals and unnecessary complications. Too much money, absence of parents from the house when the children return from school and a frivolous attitude are pushing youngsters onto this path, where they think everything is fine because they are in love. While boys may use love to get sex and girls use sex to get love, nowhere is this more evident than in adolescent relationships in which the old taboos have somewhat loosened and couples are going around and breaking up at the drop of a hat.

Eminent psychiatrist Dr Sanjay Chugh opines that sexual activity amongst school children has increased by as much as 500 per cent in recent years! "The major reasons are more openness in society, less hang-ups amongst kids themselves and, most importantly, the increase in stimulation provided to these kids by books, magazines and the Internet," says the Delhi-based psychiatrist.

Some parents frequently overlook these activities as they think they are 'cool' or 'liberal' in their outlook. But studies indicate that a female having a first-child abortion runs a five per cent risk of becoming sterile and being unable to conceive in the future. Furthermore, the stress and tension associated with clandestine sex may result in frigidity and many may not be able to have a normal sex life later on, due to diseases contracted through indiscriminate sexual activity.

The December 2001 issue of Reader's Digest has an interesting article entitled "A Parent's Guide to Teens and Sex". The article clearly advises parents to motivate their teenage children to delay sex by stressing on the moral dimension of sex, not just the physical and protective aspects, and then provide unconditional love and support so that they do not feel that sex is the only way to get this.

We would be failing in our duty as parents if, under the guise of being 'broadminded', we do not keep track of our daughter's interaction with members of the opposite sex and fail to provide her enough love, support and motivation to keep away from casual sexual relationships, which would undoubtedly have a scar on her mentally and physically.

Some Possible Solutions

- The channel of communication with one's children must be open and active at all times. No topic should be taboo and a mother should not hesitate to discuss issues like boyfriends, discos, partying and so on.

- At the school level, the child's attention should be on studies, sports and cultural activities.

- The attraction between young boys and girls should be tackled in a matter-of-fact manner. It should not be given the importance of being 'scandalous', as children are drawn like magnets towards forbidden fruit. It should be impressed upon one's daughter that it is better to wait until she is older before plunging into these complications and that there is more to life than attracting and seeking appreciation from the opposite sex. Moreover, by gaining a reputation of being 'available' and 'easy' she is unnecessarily becoming a target for abuse. One's body is something sacred and should not be used as a railway platform by casual acquaintances.

- At the college level, a girl may have a boyfriend and one should keep track of whom she is moving around with, as it is at this stage that smoking, alcohol and drugs are very alluring. One should try to see that one's daughter is with a group of friends rather than going on single dates, so as to avoid the perils of a relationship.

- Parents have to adopt a balanced approach when dealing with their daughter's mixing with the opposite sex. Extra strictness will only result in heightened 'boy craziness', while extra liberalism may have unpleasant consequences.

- The secret is to build up love, trust and self-esteem in your girl-child so that she herself is able to handle the interaction coolly and in a balanced way. Even in the 21st century there is no reason why your daughter should acquire a negative reputation or be called 'fast' or 'cheap'. The higher her self-esteem and self-confidence, the less prone will she be to compromise her dignity in any manner. Rather than making sleeping around a moral issue, it is more important to stress that one's body is something sacrosanct and others should not have easy access to it.

Valentine's Day

February 14th is celebrated as Valentine's Day all over the Western world. Valentine's Day is named after Saint Valentine, who was put to death on February 14, 269 AD in Rome. It is the day to celebrate love between couples, girlfriend and boyfriend or husband and wife. It is a day on which romance is celebrated and expressed through cards, flowers, chocolates and candlelight dinners.

Valentine's Day was virtually unknown in India a decade ago, until it came in through the flourishing greeting-card culture, a phenomenon which has taken over since globalisation began. While the Valentine concept is an imported one, it has a beneficial effect, as many Indian men are unable to express their feelings in a suave way – either they are reticent or they are crude and copy the antics of film heroes.

Seeing this public outpouring of love and romance on the streets, the Indian version of cultural policing has begun, with conservative groups trying to storm card shops to prevent the celebration of Valentine's Day, declaring it 'un-Indian'. Most people feel this is unfortunate, as it goes against the basic spirit of tolerance in the country. Celebrating Valentine's Day by merely exchanging cards or receiving a flower or bouquet from an admirer is harmless. Indian culture is too strong and deep-rooted to be shaken by one-day affairs like Valentine's Day. Love is a universal emotion and setting aside one day to celebrate it will make the world a better place to live in.

However, having said that, there is no doubt that Valentine's Day is an offshoot of globalisation, particularly in our urban centres. Such Western cultural influences are fine up to a point, but we should be careful to deal with the occasion in a balanced manner.

Dating

This is a recent phenomenon in the life of the Indian teenager. Unfortunately, the age at which it begins is getting lower and lower. It has long been a part of western culture, where it is part of the process of selecting a suitable partner. Today Indian children in Class VI and VII go on dates, sometimes with their parents' consent, but more often clandestinely. Such dates may mean eating together in the school canteen, sharing an ice-cream or pizza or even going out for a movie.

In America, there are two additional aspects to dating at a somewhat older age. One is going out on a blind date, which means going out for dinner or an outing with an unknown person. The second is the problem of date rape, in which a blind date can sometimes result in a violent encounter. An article published in the August 2001 issue of "Journal of the American Medical Association" reported that about one in five high school girls had been physically or sexually hurt by the dating partner. Not only was dating abuse ignored even in youth programmes, which were supposed to focus on problems like unwed pregnancies, addictions and their link to violence, but it was said to be a problem that occurred in all socio-economic categories.

While dating at the school level needs to be closely monitored, what with school- and college-goers frequenting 'afternoon discos', at the college level one will have to give one's daughter more freedom to go out with boys. However, parents should keep track and encourage children to go out in mixed groups rather than in exclusive duos. Sometimes a girl feels compelled to go out in a mixed group of girls and boys, so that she is not dubbed 'backward'. A certain amount of attraction and appreciation between the sexes is natural at this stage and this is what parents must keep in mind before laying down the rules.

Pornography and the Internet

The latest craze to hit young people worldwide, including India, is the Internet, e-mail and 'chatting' on the net. Many parents nag their children to stop talking on the phone and restrict their telephonic conversations with friends. Particularly where girls are concerned, parents are paranoid about boys calling and closely monitor the calls.

Today, however, children are simply using computers and the Internet to keep in touch. While parents may feel the urge to supervise this as well, making an issue of it will only result in children going out and using their friend's computer or those in a cyber cafe. Initially, all new gadgets have their own attraction and children will go on talking about them. But parents should not make any active efforts to curb this activity, as children will soon tire of it. However, any curbs at this stage will only make the child more attracted to the forbidden and they will do things clandestinely. Once the novelty has worn off, the child will then use the Internet primarily for e-mail.

A recent survey of youth aged between 15 and 24 years in the United States, published in "USA Today", revealed that they went online to procure sexual "health" information rather than to download music, play games or chat. These youngsters said they found the net important because they lacked "an already established relationship with a doctor; they want to do some exploring without anybody knowing about it", according to the author of the report, Victoria Rideout.

35

Another major danger is online pornography. Pornographic sites on the Internet have their own powerful attraction both for teenagers and others, particularly in view of our repressive and secretive attitude pertaining to sexual matters. Such sites will attract young people, despite parents' best efforts to ensure otherwise. In fact, the greater the mystery and secrecy regarding sexual matters, the greater the incentive on the part of the child to see and get information from these sites.

What Parents Can Do

If one is close to one's child one can openly discuss issues related to sex with her, so that the child can learn about the biological facts of life in a logical and matter-of-fact way and not seek clandestine sources of information.

Teenagers are always looking for information. They are eager to know about sex and hence they look to books, films and the Internet for information. Much of the information they receive surreptitiously is wrong or unscientific and this is where their problems begin – whom can they ask and how can they ask being the biggest ones. The information they generally seek pertains to conception and pregnancy, how to prevent it, what leads to Sexually Transmitted Diseases and what their symptoms are and whether masturbation is harmful or not.

Unfortunately, despite being the land of the "Kama Sutra", talking about sex has long been regarded as taboo in India, with the end result being that there is widespread ignorance. One should follow the advice of the celebrated authority, Kinsey, who said, "When parents sit on information that they should pass on to the child, the poor child starts wondering what is so secretive about it. His curiosity and interest are further increased. He begins either to think there is something shameful about his own body or he goes out to find the answers from friends. The eventual result in either case is usually bad."

Proper education is the only way to resolve this curiosity and parents, physicians and teachers have to play their role in this process. Parents must voluntarily tell children about the facts of life, as the more open parents are, the less curious and eager to experiment will children be. Proper books on sex education can be given to them so that their curiosity is satiated and their queries are answered.

The Tussle Over Television

Two or three generations ago, the bone of contention was going to the movies. Today the movies are in one's drawing room as television has virtually swamped our lives. Parents try to censor TV viewing and decide what the children can or cannot see. Some parents allow their children to watch only the Discovery and National Geographic channels.

By trying to control what your child should see on TV, one merely builds up resentment and since parents cannot always be physically present in the house, one only encourages them to watch what they want and not what you decree in your absence.

Parents are worried that their child will see something that they should not on TV, but it is not possible to protect one's child indefinitely. While one can restrict the hours that small children watch television so that they do not develop eye problems, one has to give older children greater freedom. One will gradually find that they themselves keep away from unsavoury programmes and have self-regulatory hours for watching television in-between sitting with their books.

Says an angry 14-year-old Sonal, "When my parents stop me from watching television I really get angry. After all, I know if my work is suffering or not. They don't need to keep reminding me about that."

Her friend Nisha is equally resentful: "If I am watching television my mother tells me how I could have utilised the time better by studying. It really irritates me."

One of the hazards of watching too much television – apart from eye strain and exposure to a surfeit of violence and noise – is that it leads to the couch potato syndrome wherein children plonk themselves before the idiot box, eat junk food and enjoy passive entertainment for hours on end.

Smoking, Drinking and Drugs

Indulging in smoking, drinking and taking drugs is considered a passport to adulthood. That is why, from an early age, children should be made aware of the hazards of these glamorised vices, so that by the time they grow up, they are suitably inured to their lure. Glamorous advertisements and the label of being 'modern' and 'smart' have begun luring girls from Class IX upwards into experimenting with these due to the encouragement from friends. What starts as social drinking or smoking at parties, in order to fit in with the group, soon turns into addiction.

Moreover, those girls who drink, smoke or take drugs are prone to many diseases, as they are affected by these sooner than men, whose bodies are better equipped to cope with the effects of alcohol and cigarettes. Medical research has confirmed that the ill effects of smoking and drinking affect the female body more acutely and swiftly than the male. Such girls also have more difficulty in conceiving, weight, growth and health are negatively affected.

One should be careful of the company one keeps. Sometimes, even if one does not want to booze, beverages are spiked with alcohol or drugs, making one an unwitting victim. At many parties, these methods are employed to drug the girl and molest her while she is in stupor.

Therefore, before allowing your daughter to go out for parties, ensure you know where she is going, with whom and whether you know anyone there. Also impose an appropriate curfew hour, by which time she must return home. Check her mode of transport. Rather than let her go with a group of rash drivers, when other friends are present, one could arrange for her to go in a hired taxi, so that she can return independently and within the prescribed time frame. At the school level, one could also limit the number of times she can go to parties every month.

Ultimately, how one's children cope with peer pressure and temptations that are all around is a combination of early childhood upbringing and their personal values. Parents have to instil such values in the child that even when she is exposed at the college level, she is still able to steer clear of vices.

Parents, on the other hand, have to be careful not to overdo or overreact while supervising their children. It has been found that children from the strictest and most conservative backgrounds are often the first victims of vice traps.

The Dangers of Consumerism

Traditionally, India has never had a consumerist culture and was more spiritually oriented. That is why, in the caste hierarchy, it was the man of prayers, learning and spirituality, the Brahmin, who was placed at the top of the social hierarchy, followed by the warrior-king, the Kshatriya, after which came the man of business.

Today, we are no longer able to resist the worldwide consumerist culture and have, in fact, joined it with gusto. One indicator in this regard are bride burning and dowry deaths, which still occur at regular intervals even in a city like Delhi. Statistics show that there were 13,612 dowry deaths reported in the country in 1998-99, with 6,637 brides burnt in 1999. There may be hundreds of cases that have gone unreported. We have become slaves to our possessions and consumerism is pushing us into needlessly multiplying our needs.

We have to plan our lives and train our children in such a way that we are not consumed by consumerism. It has rightly been said that the mad scramble for wealth and material possessions is as depressing as poverty.

The dividing line between a man's need and his greed is a very fine one, so unless we train ourselves to retain our balance and be content within our means, we will needlessly ruin our lives and become unhappy. Parents should be frank with their children regarding their economic status and financial commitments and not try to live beyond their means.

We should teach children the virtues and satisfaction that come from living honestly within one's means. If parents, particularly the mother, do not go on grumbling about all that they cannot afford to buy or do on the present income, then the children too will not be attracted towards an inflated lifestyle or envy their wealthy friends.

One of the unfortunate trends of modern urban life in big cities is that there is too much illicit money floating around and many ignorant parents are giving their children huge sums to spend in hotels with their friends. They are even given cars to drive, often when they are not licensed to do so.

At the college level, if not earlier in schools, such boys wish to attract friends, particularly girls, by taking them for meals to five-star hotels, to discos and so on. I remember, when I was in college nearly three decades ago, there were certain groups of fast girls who would willingly go out with boys/older men to hotels and allow their escorts certain liberties, in return for dinner at a five-star hotel or restaurant! Thus it would not be true to assert that morals have plummeted only in this generation – such things also happened in the past.

Mothers must caution their daughters against being taken in by the glib talk of wealthy boys, who can lure them to farmhouse parties and take liberties. The need to always maintain dignity and self-restraint and not be dazzled by wealth should always be underlined.

Discos, Clubs and Parties

At a certain level of affluence, particularly in urban centres, teenagers have access to discos, clubs and parties. The young have a great deal of energy, are naturally outgoing and gregarious. They often get together to celebrate birthdays, the end of exams and so on. Such celebrations and mixing on a periodic basis are quite acceptable.

The problem arises when unsavoury elements creep in and introduce drugs, drinks or start taking liberties with the girls. At recognised clubs and discos there is strict monitoring of entrants and the staff are vigilant about any public misconduct. The danger occurs when one's daughter is going to such parties in someone else's car, who may be an unlicensed, rash or drunken driver. When these parties are organised at private residences or farmhouses, certain dangers are present.

Since one would not like one's daughter to be a paranoid social recluse, one can send her to these gatherings occasionally after duly cautioning her about the perils involved. She must enjoy her youth, freedom and carefree life during the last years in school and initial years in college but parents can always give a few words of advice. A certain deadline for returning home may be imposed after mutual discussion. Any delay should be conveyed to the parents, so that there is no unnecessary worry and tension.

❈ ❈ ❈

The Role of
Physical Fitness

$\mathcal{P}$hysical fitness is extremely important once your daughter gets into her teens. This is the time when youngsters use their pocket money to gorge on junk food. With visuals of junk food being splashed over the pages of dailies or being aired on TV, thanks to aggressive advertising campaigns by McDonalds, Pizza Hut, Wimpy's and the like, teenagers think it's the in-thing to be feeding on junk food or downing morsels with Coke and Pepsi, rather than a glass of water. It is not long before excess weight begins creeping in on their waistlines.

Pizzas, burgers, French fries, pastries and other such items have nothing whatsoever to recommend them, except empty calories. Besides burning a hole in teenage pockets, such fat, oil and sugar-rich foods can lead to multiple ailments in the long run. Is it any wonder that youth in their 20s are now falling victim to early-onset (juvenile) diabetes and end up having to monitor their insulin levels every single day?

It is also not surprising to see young children's teeth chequered with cavities, thanks to the harmful habit of guzzling colas every other day, if not everyday.

Many parents complain that their children are no longer within their control and despite admonitions, continue feeding on junk food and colas. In many cases, the parents are themselves to blame, as they too are addicted to such stuff! It becomes difficult to restrain the kids when you cannot restrain yourself. If this happens to be your problem, rather than preaching what you yourself cannot practise, it would make more sense if you took some preventive measures to balance unsavoury eating habits.

The best option in such circumstances is regular exercise to keep one's body fighting fit. There are many options available and you could choose one that suits you and your teenage daughter. The options include walking, jogging, aerobics, cycling, swimming, yoga, etc. We shall, however, discuss the options purely from the angle of your teenage daughter.

Walking: This is possibly the best and safest of all options. If there is any public park near your neighbourhood, an early morning 20-to-30-minute walk five or six times a week has excellent health benefits. It keeps one's tummy in check, controls fat levels, improves stamina and endurance, besides having a host of other benefits associated with all forms of exercise. You could use canvas shoes or sandals for walking – whatever you are comfortable with.

The amount of calories you burn per day through this form of exercise will depend on your walking speed and the total time spent (for total calories burnt, see the Calorie Chart). Experts recommend that one alternate between a fast and moderate speed. That is, walk at a moderate pace for five or ten minutes; then a fast pace for five or ten minutes; then again at a moderate pace. However, if you are more comfortable walking at a specific pace only, do just that.

You could also spend some time walking barefoot on grass, which is considered to have more therapeutic benefits, as it directly stimulates various nerves connected to the soles

43

of the feet. The best thing about walking is that there are no harmful effects whatsoever.

Calorie Chart
(Calories burnt in various activities)

	Activity	Cal. expenditure per minute
1.	Laying still	1.0
2.	Sitting, standing, reading, writing,	1.5
3.	Driving a car, tailoring	2.0
4.	Washing floors, sweeping and ironing	2.2
5.	Golf	2.5
6.	Walking @ 5 km per hour	3.0
7.	Walking @ 7 km per hour	4.5
8.	Walking @ 9 km per hour	9.0
9.	Gardening, weeding etc	5.0
10.	Cycling (depending upon speed)	3.5 to 8.0
11.	Boxing, rowing	12.0
12.	Dancing	5.0
13.	Table tennis	5.5
14.	Tennis	6.0
15.	Swimming @ 3 km per hour	9.0
16.	Football	8.0
17.	Running (depending upon speed)	10 to 25
18.	Other exercises:	
	a) Light	2.5
	b) Moderate	4.0
	c) Heavy	8.0

Jogging: Those looking for a more strenuous form of exercise could consider jogging. Like walking, this too is best done in the early morning hours. It is best to use canvas or sports shoes for this purpose. Besides, as far as possible, it is safer to jog over a grass or sand track, rather than a concrete surface. Jogging over a concrete surface could lead to shin and joint problems in the long run.

You could burn up a lot more calories through jogging than walking. Having said that, however, be warned that jogging is a high-impact activity that could lead to some problems. For instance, a regular early morning jog without properly warming up could lead to swelling of the feet. So, before getting into your stride, ensure at least half an hour of walking and other activities to get the blood flowing after a long night's sleep.

The other bad effect some people report is that over a sustained period of time, jogging makes one look haggard. So, despite the extra calories it burns vis-à-vis walking, jogging may not be the best option for your daughter on a regular basis.

Aerobics: Literally, the word aerobic denotes "with oxygen" or "in the presence of oxygen". Aerobic exercise is any activity that uses large muscle groups, which can be done continuously for a long period of time and is rhythmic in nature. Aerobics helps the heart, lungs and cardiovascular system process and deliver oxygen more quickly and efficiently to every part of the body. As the heart muscle becomes stronger and more efficient, a larger amount of blood is pumped with each stroke. This means that fewer strokes are required to rapidly transport oxygen to all parts of the body. An aerobically fit individual can work longer, more vigorously and achieve a quicker recovery at the end of each aerobic session.

Like all forms of exercise, it has multiple health benefits. However, like jogging, many aerobic exercises include high-impact movements that could lead to injuries, if not done under proper supervision and after warming up adequately. In fact, jogging itself is a form of aerobic activity. Ensure your daughter practises aerobics under a qualified trainer and performs the warm-up and cool-down exercises, the latter being as important as the former in preventing soreness and injury.

Another way out is to practise low-impact aerobics, where one does movements without jumping and jarring the rest of the body.

Cycling: An excellent way to increase endurance and keep fit. Cycling at 20 km per hour is a good way to work up a sweat. However, it is the muscles of the lower body that are directly exercised.

Swimming: This is the only form of exercise that ensures a workout for almost the entire body, including the eyes. But one must never swim on a full stomach, as this increases the risk of a heart attack. A light snack is allowed, however, especially if you are swimming in a river. This is because if one swallows some contaminated water accidentally, it lowers the risk of paratyphoid. This risk is not present in chlorinated swimming pools, though.

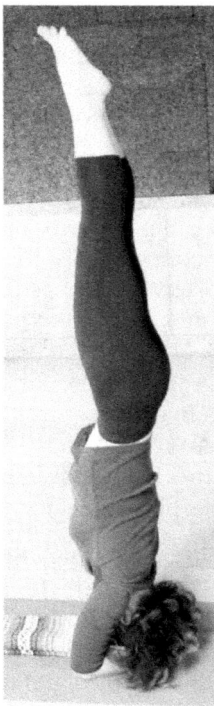

The downside on swimming is that it leads to a marked darkening of the skin. However, the skin gradually returns to its normal colour once swimming is discontinued. All in all, it is one of the best forms of exercise.

Yoga: The world's best, most comprehensive system of exercise, yoga has innumerable benefits. It cures, controls or prevents anxiety, asthma, arthritis, blood pressure, back pain, chronic fatigue, depression, diabetes, epilepsy, headaches, heart disease and a host of other ailments. Of course, your daughter wouldn't be having these diseases at such a young age! However, there would be other direct benefits for her, as yoga:

46

- Improves muscle tone, flexibility, strength and stamina
- Lowers fat
- Stimulates the immune system
- Reduces stress and tension
- Boosts self-esteem
- Improves concentration and creativity
- Improves circulation
- Creates a sense of well-being and calm.

Do bear in mind though, that yoga should be practiced under the guidance of a trained person, as there could be harmful effects if it is done incorrectly.

These are just some of the popular forms of exercise that we have outlined. There are other forms of exercise too, especially sports, which could ensure your daughter stays fit as a fiddle. If your daughter is the sports-loving kind, she could indulge herself at the school, college or residential sports club. Badminton, lawn tennis, table tennis, volleyball and cricket are just some of the games that could ensure a good workout for your daughter.

A note of caution! If your daughter has not been exercising before, she should initially restrict the duration to just 20 minutes, irrespective of the form of exercise. After a couple of weeks, the duration could be gradually raised, when her body is used to exercising. During the workout session, if there is any feeling of discomfort or pain, she should take a break immediately and rest for a while. Exercise is not recommended during periods of illness. She could, however, exercise during her menses if it doesn't cause her any extra discomfort. In fact, her menses would be less painful, problematic or prolonged if she exercises regularly.

Do also ensure that she wears loose, comfortable clothes while working out, preferably cotton, since it absorbs sweat better than synthetic garments.

Remember – there is no better way to prevent disease and retard ageing than exercise.

With fitness being part of what is regarded as 'beauty', women are working out not only to look and feel better, but also to develop endurance, energy and stamina as they challenge male domains. As they sculpt their bodies to keep pace with their demanding lives, many are turning to yoga to combat the aches and pains which result from sitting for hours before their computer. Professional life is highly competitive, hence one has to be in good health in order to be part of the race. Thus, a balanced diet and a correct balance of rest, exercise and some vitamin supplements will stand your daughter in good stead in the years ahead when she balances her life as a wife, a mother and a professional.

❀ ❀ ❀

Emotional
Well-being

6

When your daughter enters the teens, one of the most important factors that will stand her in good stead throughout her personal and professional life is her emotional strength and well-being. Being emotionally resilient can make all the difference between winning and losing. It can also make the impossible possible.

But this will not happen all by itself. The right emotions also have to be fostered and fine-tuned, just the way one would do with one's body to ensure its well-being. It is very important for your daughter to know how and when to express her emotions. And how and when to refrain from expressing her emotions and controlling them, instead. All this is a fine art, though, which will take time in mastering.

The teenage years are a time when girls are likely to fall in and out of love! Sometimes at the drop of a hat! This is natural and nothing for you to be alarmed about. Which is not to say that you don't take precautionary measures. To begin with, it is necessary for you to make your daughter understand the difference between love and infatuation. The emotion that a young girl most often feels for her teacher or professor is nothing but infatuation, a passing teenage crush. At this stage, though, your daughter will be convinced this is the real thing – this is her Mr Right. Except for the object of her affection, nothing else may seemingly matter.

Mother's Guile

This is the time for you to use all your guile and play it cool. Openly trying to dissuade her from this infatuation – which is

49

what it is, you realise with all your hard-boiled experience – will be counterproductive. The more you try to pull her away, the more strongly will she be attracted to the man. Rather than ticking her off for the crush, you would be better off seemingly teaching her some "tricks of the trade" and making her think you are on "her side"! So play along.

The first thing she should be told is that she must never ever wear her heart on her sleeve. Tell your daughter that making her affection clear to the man (or boy, as the case may be) will only make her seem so "gettable", "approachable" and "cheap". The charm of a girl lies in her inaccessibility and unavailability. For this, she has to play hard-to-get – even if that's the last thing she's feeling.

Such a shrewd tactic on your part has many benefits. Firstly, if the man hasn't already sensed your daughter has a crush on him (he probably may have already cottoned onto her feelings!), it makes the chances of him realising this, thereafter, all the more difficult.

Secondly, it introduces the element of time, thwarting or delaying the chances of anything happening between your daughter and her supposed "heart throb". There's nothing like playing for time in such situations. More often than not, she may simply outgrow the infatuation over the days, weeks or months. She may suddenly realise that she no longer "loves" that guy, but is actually in love with Aamir or Shah Rukh Khan! Which would be all for the better, as these film stars wouldn't pose a threat to your peace of mind or your daughter's chastity!

Thirdly, even if the guy reciprocates her "love", the chances of the affair taking off immediately are somewhat dim. Don't forget – the smart mother that you are, you have taught your daughter how to play hard-to-get! This again buys you more time to add some other spoke in the love wheel; of course, without your daughter getting wise to what you are up to. Remember – you are on "her side"! These lessons ensure no Romeo will be able to easily take advantage of her naiveté and take your daughter for a ride.

If things do not go your way, however, and your daughter is involved with some Tom, Dick or Harry teaching her to be emotionally resilient is still important. More often than not, such affairs fizzle out before long, with the girls left jilted and nursing broken hearts. If this happens with your daughter, this may seem like the end of the road, and the world, for her.

You know it is not! You have to quickly convey this very fact to her. And lot's more... A boy who has jilted her is not worth the tears and heartache she is putting herself through. There are many other fish in the sea – better ones at that. All that happens, happens for the best. Any guy who deserted her didn't deserve her in the first place! Finally, she is really lucky that a jerk like this guy is no longer in her life, because he wasn't the right person for her anyway. Mr Right has yet to arrive. And so on.

By constantly reinforcing her spirits with positive thoughts, you will help your daughter hold herself together and pull through emotionally. At such delicate moments in life, it is control of the mind that matters. If she can manage this, she will always be her own master (mistress if you please!). This will also ensure she does not slip into a slough of despondance or despair, nor flirt with a nervous breakdown. At her age, that's the last thing she should be flirting with, anyway!

Emotional resilience is not just important for her personal life. It can make all the difference between success and failure in the professional sphere too. An emotionally strong person is better able to command respect, win support from peers and colleagues, motivate better performance from herself and subordinates and achieve excellence in her professional life.

Expressing Oneself

Of course, make it clear to your daughter that being emotionally tough and resilient does not mean that one should not express one's feelings in weaker moments, pretending one is hard as nails. Such an attempt to bottle up emotions will be futile and counterproductive.

There will be moments in life when your daughter feels low and there may or may not be any valid or apparent reason for this. At such times, she may feel like simply bursting into tears. Tell her to go right ahead! More often than not, the spontaneous release of tears tends to have a cathartic effect. When something is wrong, trying to suppress her emotions will only lead to problems, physical as well as mental, later on. In such a scenario, it is better your daughter cries and unburdens herself, rather than pretends everything is hunky-dory. Of course, she is better off doing this in the confines of her home or room.

Inculcating such a pragmatic attitude in her will also ensure that she is comfortable in sharing her problems with you, since she knows you will not berate her for "shedding useless tears". So, while emotional resilience would require her to be smart and not expose her feelings to all and sundry, at home she should discuss her ups and downs with you. For you don't just have to be her mother, you also have to be your daughter's good friend, if not her best friend. Once she feels you stand by her through thick and thin, she will feel emotionally secure through all phases of her life, good, bad or indifferent.

In short, your daughter should be taught that in life one has to maintain a healthy balance between emotion and rational thought. There may be times when one has to go by what the brain says. At other times, one has to listen to one's heart. Maintaining this fine balance is an art. But once you stress the importance of this and give her the necessary guidelines, she will ultimately learn when to follow her head – and when to follow her heart... not her heartthrob!

❀ ❀ ❀

Handling Puberty
and its Problems

$\mathcal{P}$uberty is the most tumultuous period of hormonal change in girls and boys. It is a time of tremendous emotional, physical and mental upheaval and requires a concerted effort on the part of the mother and daughter to get through the period as a normal phase of life. Generally, adolescence starts when the individual attains sexual maturity and ends when independence from parental authority is assured. Since the age of sexual maturing varies, it is difficult to delineate the period of adolescence.

Adolescence refers to all stages of maturing, while puberty relates to sexual maturing only. While the period of adolescence may be said to be between 14 and 18 years for boys and 13 to 18 years for girls, puberty is an overlapping period. Out of an average of four years, about two are spent in preparing for the body reproduction (this period overlaps the end of childhood, the so-called pre-adolescence and pubescence). The remaining two years are spent in completing the process. To know what the hormonal changes entail, one needs to understand the complex process that goes on in the adolescent body.

The Physical Changes

For most girls the development of breasts is the first physical sign of puberty. However, for some girls it is the appearance of pubic hair that heralds puberty. The development of breasts is stimulated by ovarian activity and the production of the hormone, oestrogen. For this to occur, the area in the brain called the hypothalamus has to mature and send out steady hormone messages to the pituitary gland in the brain. This, in turn, has to produce enough FSH (Follicle Stimulating Hormone) to get the follicles present in the ovaries to develop and produce oestrogen.

Besides, oestrogen also promotes fat accumulation in the hips, thighs and buttocks, so that body curves appear. It also changes and thickens the vaginal wall, causes the uterus to mature and grow and also the cervix to produce mucous. This results in a light yellow tinged discharge and many confuse it with an infection. Some adolescent girls are so horrified with this that they start hiding their panties in shame and suffer psychological trauma.

Just before, or about the same time, a second group of hormones produced by the adrenal glands are pushed into production by the hypothalamus and pituitary glands. These are the male-like hormones called DHEA and androstenedione. They stimulate growth of pubic hair, followed by hair in the underarms. The testosterone-like qualities of these hormones also cause girls to develop acne, perspire and acquire body odour.

Most often, adolescent girls who suffer from body odour develop an inferiority complex and use all kinds of cosmetic products to overcome the odour. An intelligent mother should be able to instill a sense of security in her daughter by pointing out that it is a natural outcome of being a teenager. The emergence of acne also disturbs the teenager and the mother could alleviate her concerns by being supportive and trying various herbal methods to combat the problem.

This phase, activated by the adrenals, is called the adrenarche. Incidentally, these male hormones are also responsible for developing sexual interest of girls in males. Meanwhile, a third hormonal upheaval occurs simultaneously. It is the increased production of growth hormone, which interacts with many other crucial hormones such as insulin, thyroid, adrenal and sex hormones, causing a spurt in growth of bones and organs. During this spurt, height increases about three and a half inches each year and this usually continues from the beginning of breast development until the onset of periods. Once the menstrual cycles are regular, most girls add just two or more inches to their height and stop growing between the ages of 16 and 18.

As girls grow taller and their body fat nearly doubles, they gain an average of seven to nine kilos over a two-to-three-year period. This is generally known as puppy fat, which normally sheds by itself in a few years. Sometimes, this spurt in body weight can also have psychological effects in an adolescent daughter. She has to be reassured that it is a passing phase.

The last major physical sign of puberty is menarche, or the first period. The follicles in the ovaries finally reach maturity. Both the hormones, oestrogen and progesterone, are released and cause the uterine lining to become thick and after two weeks, if no pregnancy occurs, the hormone level drops and the lining sheds. This is the first period. Once it starts, however, this complicated hormonal system may still have inconsistencies. So periods are often irregular for the first two years after menarche.

With changes in dietary habits and other environmental factors, the average age of menarche has reduced greatly in the past decade. Some girls have their menarche at a comparatively early age and is called precocious puberty. A child may suffer from anxiety because her peers have not begun menstruating. This is a crucial period and the mother has to act as a counsellor and guide to her daughter by explaining that it is quite normal and nothing to get upset about.

On the other hand, some girls have late menarche. Although the age for menarche can vary from 11 to 15, some girls who do not menstruate till late feel quite troubled since most of their friends are in the stage of menarche. In such cases, a mother should counsel and reassure her that it is normal for a variation in the age group to occur. Consulting a doctor could also reassure the teenager.

A teenaged girl will also be worried about the state of her skin during this time. The skin may get oilier and pimples could appear. It is important to clean the skin and use a deodorant or antiperspirant on underarms to keep odour and wetness under control.

Despite best efforts, pimples will keep appearing because of hormonal changes.

Emotional Changes

In addition to the many physical changes that occur during puberty, there are many emotional changes as well. The teenager may start to care more about what other people think about her and would want to be accepted and liked. At this time, relationships with others may begin to change. Some become more important and others less so. The adolescent begins to move away from the parents and identify with others of her age. She may begin to take decisions that could affect the rest of her life.

Many girls of adolescent age feel self-conscious about their changing appearances – too tall, too short, too fat, or too skinny. Because puberty causes so many changes, it is hard not to compare what is going on with one's body to what is happening to one's friends' bodies. The mother has to repeatedly assure the daughter that everyone goes through puberty differently and, eventually, everyone catches up.

The insecurity and uncertainties that hound an adolescent may not appear very serious to adults, but for them it is a very serious matter. Gentle counselling and guidance at every stage could help the adolescent emerge with a healthy attitude about the entire process.

This is also the time that sex education becomes imperative and mothers should warn the child about the hazards of sexual adventures. Peer pressure and media glorification are some factors that could lead a teenager to experiment with unknown but exciting zones.

Discussing Sex

It is important to talk about the responsibilities and consequences that come from being sexually active. Pregnancy, sexually transmitted diseases, and feelings about sex are important issues to be discussed. Talking to your children can help them make the decisions that are best for them without feeling pressured to do something before they are ready.

Helping children understand that these are decisions that require maturity and responsibility will increase the chances that they make good choices.

Adolescents are able to talk about lovemaking and sex in terms of dating and relationships. They may need help dealing with the intensity of their own sexual feelings, confusion regarding their sexual identity and behaviour in a relationship. Concerns regarding masturbation, menstruation, contraception, pregnancy, and sexually transmitted diseases are common.

Some adolescents also struggle with conflicts around family, religious or cultural values. Open communication and accurate information from parents increase the likelihood that teenagers will curb their desire to experiment with sex.

In talking with your adolescent daughter, it is helpful to:

● Encourage your child to talk and ask questions.

● Maintain a calm and non-critical atmosphere for discussions.

● Use words that are understandable and comfortable.

● Try to determine your child's level of knowledge and understanding. Keep your sense of humour and don't be afraid to talk about your own discomfort.

● Relate sex to love, intimacy, caring, and respect for oneself and one's partner.

● Be open in sharing your values and concerns.

● Discuss the importance of responsibility for choices and decisions.

● Help your child consider the pros and cons of choices.

By developing open, honest and ongoing communication about responsibility, sex, and choice, parents can help their youngsters learn about sex in a healthy and positive manner.

Some Useful Tips

- You should talk to your teenager about the changes that their bodies are going to go through before the onset of puberty so that they are not surprised by these changes. Your daughter should understand that these changes are normal and there is nothing to get worried about.

- Every mother must educate her adolescent daughter and prepare her gently for what lies ahead. Initially the periods may be scanty or heavy, may occur at three-week or six-week intervals and may be painful or painless.

- A mother must also guide her adolescent daughter about the use and proper disposal of a sanitary napkin, which must always be wrapped in paper and put in a paper or plastic packet before being thrown.

- Adopt a positive and matter-of-fact attitude towards menstruation, which is a perfectly natural phenomenon and a vitally important part of a woman's physical well-being. It is neither an illness nor a painful and uncomfortable time for everyone. A high-strung personality, an illness or anxiety may lead to very heavy blood loss or to skipping of the period, which is why girls need to have an equable temperament and attitude for their physical welfare.

Puberty is also the time when a mother should be well equipped to handle all kinds of emotional and psychological problems that may arise. A well-informed and intelligent mother is more likely to sail comfortably out of the choppy waters with her daughter in tow.

❀ ❀ ❀

SELF-IMPROVEMENT/PERSONALITY DEVELOPMENT

Also Available in Hindi

Also Available in Hindi

Also Available in Kannada, Tamil

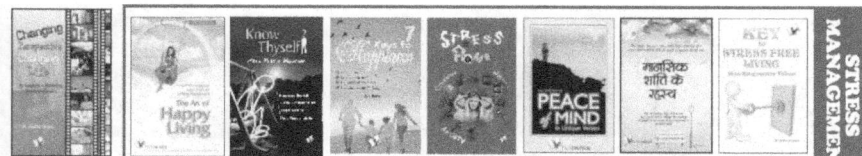

Also Available in Kannada

Also Available in Kannada

All books available at www.vspublishers.com

HINDI LITERATURE

TALES & STORIES

All Books Fully Coloured

MUSIC/MYSTERIES/MAGIC & FACT

OTHER BOOKS

CHILDREN TALES (बच्चों की कहानियाँ)

Folk Tales   Interesting Tales   Jungle Tales   Legendary Tales   Ramayana Tales

BANGLA LANGUAGE (बांग्ला भाषा)

All books available at **www.vspublishers.com**

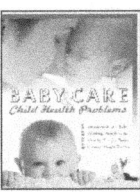